Gourock
Then & Now

John Fyfe Anderson

Haymaking on the high ground above Gourock. Kempock point can be seen in the background on the extreme right of the town. In the mid-nineteenth century on both sides of Kempock Point there were green fields which stretched along the foot of the hill and the original fishing village consisted of a few scattered houses surrounding Gourock Bay. Gourock expanded by gradually moving up the hillside on both its eastern and western flanks. It now extends for two miles along the shore on either side of Kempock Point. The boundaries of Gourock were originally established in 1858 and extended in 1924 when the area was increased by 242 acres. In 1935 a further 13 acres were added and by 1959 the total area of Gourock amounted to 626 acres. As a result of more houses being built in the town, the number of farms has been reduced. In 1914 there were 341 acres of farmland but by 1959 it was just over 60 acres. The site of this haymaking is now rough, uncultivated ground.

Text © John Fyfe Anderson, 2020.
First published in the United Kingdom, 2020, reprinted 2025
by Stenlake Publishing Ltd.,
54-58 Mill Square,
Catrine, Ayrshire,
KA5 6RD

Telephone: 01290 551122
www.stenlake.co.uk

ISBN 9781840338744

Printed by P2D,
1 Newlands Road,
Westoning,
MK45 5LD

The publishers regret that they cannot supply copies of any pictures featured in this book.

Acknowledgements

The assistance of Fumi Nakabachi and Yushin Toda in photographing present day Gourock is gratefully acknowledged. Thanks are also due to Gourock Heritage and Arts for assistance.

Further Reading

The books listed below were used by the author during his research. Only Old Gourock is available from Stenlake Publishing. Those interested in finding out more are advised to contact their local bookshop or reference library.

MacDougall, S. and Monteith, J., *Gourock, Inverkip and Wemyss Bay from Old Photographs*, 1981.
McCrorie, J., *To The Coast. One Hundred Years of the Caledonian Steam Packet Company*, 1989.
Milne, C., *The Story of Gourock 1858-1958*, 1958.
Paterson, A.J.S., *The Victorian Summer of the Clyde Steamers 1864-1888*, 2001.
Paterson, A.J.S., *The Golden Years of the Clyde Steamers, 1899-1914*, 1979.
Twaddle, G., *Old Gourock*, 1999.
Walker, F. A., *The South Clyde Estuary, An Illustrated Guide to Inverclyde and Renfrew*, 1986.
'The Burgh of Gourock', *The Third Statistical Account of Scotland*, 1959.
The Greenock Telegraph
The Gourock Times

Introduction

Gourock is situated on the shores of the Firth of Clyde, 28 miles west of Glasgow at a point opposite the entrance to Loch Long. The name is believed to be derived from two Celtic words meaning 'circular bay'.

The estate of Gourock was originally owned by the Earls of Douglas but in 1455 King James II granted it to Sir David Stewart of Castlemilk. In the town's early days fishing was the main industry. In 1688 Walter Gibson of Cardwell Bay was recorded as an early proponent of curing kippers, or 'red herrings' as they were once known, and in the eighteenth century a number of families from the north of Scotland came to live in the town, attracted by the good fishing.

A charter of 1695 made Gourock a burgh of barony which meant that it had the right to hold a weekly market and two fairs per year, one in June and one in November. However, in spite of this, Gourock did not grow significantly and continued as a small fishing village, although there were a few other minor industries such as boatbuilding, quarrying, mining and a ropeworks.

In 1784 the Stewarts sold the estate for £15,000 to Duncan Darroch, a plantation owner in Jamaica, and by this time Gourock was becoming popular as a holiday resort; into the nineteenth century, tourism would become a mainstay of the local economy, especially with the opening of the railway to Greenock in 1841.

Gourock became a police burgh in 1858 and the elected town council became responsible for local services such as policing, paving, lighting and cleansing. By 1880 Gourock had a police station, a rifle corps (the 22nd Renfrewshire), a coastguard station, a post office with telegraph facilities and a post office savings bank. There was also a Freemasons' lodge and a floral and horticultural society and also bowling, curling, skating, sailing and cricket clubs.

The development of transport facilities, the growth of shipbuilding on the River Clyde at Greenock and Port Glasgow along with the increase in wealth in the west of Scotland were all factors which contributed to the growth of Gourock between 1850 and 1900. The railway was extended to Gourock pier in 1889, making the town even more accessible. Businessmen from Glasgow and increasing numbers of higher-paid workers in Greenock and Port Glasgow came to live in Gourock. By 1881 the population of the burgh was 3,336, increasing to 5,261 by 1901.

Even before the railway was extended there were steamer connections and Tweed's *Guide to Glasgow and the Clyde* of 1872 stated that 'the pier at Gourock was crowded with folks waiting for friends from Glasgow', continuing: 'Gourock is the first real watering-place which a steamer direct from Glasgow reaches and as such is much frequented by those to whom rapid and cheap access is of importance. It is popular with the working classes who for the most part put up in the east quarter of the town'.

In the Renfrewshire County Handbook of the mid 1950s it is mentioned that 'if the perfect holiday resort exists, Gourock has a bigger claim to the title than most places as it had all the facilities which any holiday-maker could desire'. However, by then its popularity as a holiday resort was in decline. Writing in the *Third Statistical Account of Scotland* in 1959, the Rev. William Caskie stated: 'It is no longer the case that the population (of Gourock) is doubled or trebled in the summer months'. However, Gourock's significance as a holiday resort, especially for Glaswegians, cannot be forgotten and on the site of the former pierhead buildings there is a statue of 'The Girl on the Suitcase', affectionately known as 'Wee Annie'. This statue was commissioned by Riverside Inverclyde to commemorate Gourock's former importance as a major holiday resort and an embarkation point for River Clyde steamers.

Today the town is a pleasant residential area with a modern railway station and ferry service. It is still a popular place for day-trippers. The most recent population estimate is 10,350, having declined from 11,561 in 2001. In 1959 the Rev. Caskie also wrote: 'Gourock's popularity as a most delightful place to live is never likely to be eclipsed' – a statement that is as true now as it was then.

A view of Gourock showing Cardwell Bay and Kempock Point from Lyle Road, Greenock, taken in October 1938. In 1880 the only house west of Kempock Point was a small farm cottage. However, by the late 1950s houses had been built further up the hillside in Gourock and along the seafront on both the east and west sides of Kempock Point. During the Second World War, Gourock had an important role in the war effort. The assembly point for numerous convoys of ships was near Gourock pier and many ships which had been torpedoed were brought to the town for repair. The liner *Queen Elizabeth* made

34 return crossings as a troopship between Gourock and New York between 1942 and 1945; Prime Minister Winston Churchill was a regular passenger on that great ship. During the war many men who were serving in the armed forces were based in or near Gourock and their families came to live in the town for the duration of the conflict. More houses have since been built over on the left of this scene. In the foreground there are now trees and bushes and the road shown here no longer exists.

TORPEDO WORKS, NEAR GOUROCK.

In 1907 the Admiralty compulsorily purchased land at the Battery Park in Greenock from Sir Hugh Shaw Stewart for £27,225 in order to erect the Royal Naval Torpedo Factory which was just over the boundary from Gourock and can be seen here on the shore, towards the upper left of the photograph. The site of the factory covered 10 acres of land and 4.75 acres of foreshore with the cost of its construction being in the region of £30,000. The manufacture of torpedoes began in 1910 when 700 workers from the Royal Arsenal in Woolwich, London, came to work in the factory. Before coming to Greenock a deputation of workers visited Gourock and were very satisfied with its quality of housing and the new senior school in Binnie Street. Houses were built in the town to accommodate these workers and these houses were in Nelson Road, Rodney Road, Grenville Road and Collingwood Road, all named after

British admirals. The increase in the population of Gourock from 5,261 in 1901 to 7,442 in 1911 was in large measure due to the influx of workers from Woolwich. In 1959 the Rev. William C. Caskie, writer of the *Third Statistical Account of Scotland* entry for the Burgh of Gourock, stated that the 'Woolwichers' and their descendants at that time formed a substantial part of the town's population. During and after the First World War the design and manufacture of torpedoes took place in the factory but design work ceased on the outbreak of the Second World War and all efforts were concentrated on manufacture. The buildings of the Fort Matilda Industrial Park are now located on the site of the former torpedo factory.

This is a view of the first golf course and clubhouse in Gourock. It was located on Midton and Divert farms. Duncan Darroch, the local landowner and 4th Baron of Gourock, had agreed to give the club the area required for a nine-hole course, which was laid out by Frank Macdonald. It opened on 13 June 1896 with a large gathering in attendance. The Rev. A Milne, captain of the newly formed Gourock Golf Club, announced that the club already had 60 members

of whom fifteen were ladies. Before opening the course for play, Duncan Darroch, the eldest son of the landowner, was presented with a very fine driver which bore an inscription in silver commemorating the opening. He then drove the ball with his new club from the first tee. The clubhouse has been demolished and there is now no open space as a result of housing development in Golf Road and Kirn Drive.

Designed by James Miller, Gourock Railway Station was originally built for the Caledonian Railway Company because it was losing business in the Clyde steamer trade to the new Glasgow and South Western Terminal at Prince's Pier in Greenock. A new railway line was laid through a tunnel to Gourock where a pier was built for the steamers. The cost of this railway line was £620,000. It was officially opened on 1 June 1889 and the first regular train left Gourock at 05:25, bringing workmen to Greenock and Port Glasgow. The first train from Glasgow on that day arrived in Gourock at 07:21. The Caledonian Steam Packet Company's *Ivanhoe* was the first steamer to berth at Gourock pier on the same day. In the period from 1 June to 31 December 1889 almost

700,000 passengers travelled on the railway line from Greenock to Gourock. In 2006 renovation of the station took place with the provision of a new entrance, glass roof, toilets and improved waiting facilities. A new station building designed by IDP Architects was in use by the end of 2010. During 2011 the existing glazed canopies on the platforms were demolished and new shelters were erected. The new station building was officially opened by Alex Neil MSP on 1 August 2012. The total cost of all the building work was £8 million. There is now a landscaped walkway from Shore Street to the station.

The first quay in Gourock was located opposite the bottom of Hopeton Street. It was replaced in 1840 by a new quay a short distance to the west which was able to accommodate steamers such as *Eagle 2*, seen here at the quay in 1871. This steamer was built at Charles Connell and Company's shipbuilding yard at Overnewton, Glasgow, and was launched there on 25 April 1864. She was an impressive sight with two funnels forward of the paddleboxes and a raised quarter-deck in order to provide improved light and ventilation in the main saloon in the stern. A newspaper report stated that the vessel had 'been elegantly fitted up and every modern improvement introduced for the comfort of passengers'. There was even a piano on board for those 'who are musically inclined'. *Eagle 2* was delivered to Captain William Buchanan for the Rothesay service from the Broomielaw, Glasgow, early in June 1864. Her first engines

were provided by the Anchor Line which at one time was well known in the Finnieston district of Glasgow. In 1866 the steamer underwent extensive alterations when the hull was lengthened by sixteen feet behind the paddleboxes to improve her performance. Further alterations took place in 1877 with a complete rebuilding and the installation of one haystack boiler and a new single diagonal engine replacing the original double engines. After this renovation *Eagle 2* only had one funnel and sailed on Clyde waters until 1894 when she was sold; she was broken up in 1899. There is no longer a quay in this location; the building on the right is Gourock railway station.

A new Cove Road Esplanade was opened in September 1899. It was built in order to prevent further damage to the roadway because of heavy tides. The esplanade was considered to be a great improvement on the previous one's narrow and poor condition. After its completion the new esplanade was described as 'double its normal width, with clear comfortable sidewalks and grassy plots with rows of shady trees and seats for weary pedestrians making

that part of Gourock into a most desirable residential district'. Cove Road was originally known as Ropework Street as this was where the Gourock Ropework Company was located. This company was founded in 1711 and was renowned throughout the world for the manufacture of ropes, canvas, tarpaulin and sailcloth. It moved to Port Glasgow in 1851 and closed in 1976.

This is Cardwell Road in 1928 with the tramlines still in place. On the extreme left is the distinctive domed tenement at 72 Cardwell Road which was built around 1890. It is located near the boundary of Gourock and Greenock. There are Art Nouveau tiles in the tenement closes at 58-70 Cardwell Road. Both Cardwell Road and Cardwell Bay are named after Edward Cardwell (1813-1886), a nineteenth-century British politician who was elevated to the peerage as 1st Viscount Cardwell. He held office as President of the Board of Trade from 1852 to 1855 and also as Secretary of State for the Colonies from 1864 to

1866. As Secretary of State of War from 1868 to 1874 he abolished the purchase of officers' commissions in the army. Cardwell's connection with Gourock was a result of his marriage to Anne Parker who was the younger sister of Mrs Susan Darroch of Gourock, wife of Duncan Darroch, 3rd Baron of Gourock (1829-1889). The view is remarkably similar today, apart from changes in the shops and street furniture and the removal of the building on the left whose gable end is just behind the car.

CARDWELL ROAD. GOUROCK.

This is a view of Cardwell Road looking east in the 1920s. On the left there are the premises of a stationer and tobacconist with a notice outside advertising that it was possible to use the phone inside the shop. In the 1920s only a minority of the population had phones in their own homes. The detached houses in this photograph are well built and exhibit a measure of the prosperity of Gourock. Gourock merges with Greenock near this location in Cardwell Road.

In 1927 Greenock Town Council presented the Greenock Burgh Extension Bill to Parliament with the proposal that it should annex the burghs of Port Glasgow and Gourock. However, the people of Port Glasgow and Gourock were strongly against this proposal and the Bill was rejected by a parliamentary select committee and Greenock lost its case.

This is the scene in a quiet and almost traffic-free Cardwell Road in September 1931, just two years after the electric tram service had ceased to operate. Cardwell Road was originally lit by gas and lamp-posts can be seen on both sides. Gourock was first lit by gas in 1849 when the gas works – the first in

any of the towns on the Clyde Coast – were operated by a small private company. Gourock Town Council became responsible for the gas works in 1884. All gas street lighting in the town was replaced by electricity in the 1950s.

Gourock Steam Laundry on Cardwell Road was founded in 1897 by three men from Gourock and originally there were about 35 shareholders. The business changed hands a number of times over the years, the last occasion being in 1945 when it was taken over by the Rodger family who owned it until closure in 1958. A report in the *Greenock Telegraph* of 2 February 1958 announced that the laundry would close within two weeks; it had a workforce of 48, 33 of whom were women and girls. The only job that would be saved was that of a van driver who would be employed by the business which was taking over

the delivery runs of the laundry. John Rodger, the managing director, stated in the report that most small laundry businesses in Scotland were losing money: people were not sending items to laundries as they once did mainly because of the increasing ownership of washing machines, spin dryers and the advent of non-iron fabrics. Nothing now remains of the laundry and flats have been built on the site.

A traffic-free scene looking from Broomberry Drive in January 1929. Larkfield Road is on the right with Chapel Street on the left. The house on the right, probably a gate lodge for Gourock House, has been demolished while the tenements on the left in Cardwell Road remain in position. Also on the right, but out of site round the corner, is the entrance to Gourock Park. The Darroch family tomb is situated within Gourock Park near the former site of Gourock

House. Darroch Park, which is separated from Gourock Park by Broomberry Drive, is now the site of Gourock Primary School which has been there since 1999 after relocating from Binnie Street.

Gourock House was built for the Stewarts of Castlemilk in 1747 near the site of Gourock Castle which had been demolished. In 1784 Duncan Darroch, an owner of a West Indies plantation, purchased the Barony of Gourock for £15,000 from the Stewarts. There is a story that, as a young boy, Darroch climbed into the garden of Gourock House with the intention of stealing apples from the orchard, and when he was chased out by the gardener he vowed that one day he would return to buy the estate. In 1913 one of his descendants, Lieut. Colonel Duncan Darroch, donated five acres of his land to Gourock Town

Council. This became known as Darroch Park which was located half-a-mile south-east of the town centre and provided an open space for sports and football. In 1923 the Town Council purchased Gourock House and grounds from the Lieut. Colonel for £10,075 and the grounds became known as Gourock Park. Gourock House was demolished in 1946. A walled garden remains in the park which also has facilities such as a bowling club, tennis courts, two grass football pitches, a cricket square and a pavilion.

The gentleman in the suit seen in this photograph may be the owner of the business himself. Note the delivery handcart on the right.

There is now a high rise apartment block on the site of Forbes' premises, located in Chapel Street.

The drapery business of G. Millar and Sons was located in Shore Street. In 1959 there were 211 shops in Gourock. In that year the writer of the entry for the Burgh of Gourock in the *Third Statistical Account of Scotland* stated the following: 'The number and variety of shops meet the requirements of the community and there is little need to go outside for normal shopping expeditions.'

A block of flats now stands on the site of Millar's premises.

A well-dressed lady faces the photographers in Barrhill Road. Both of the houses with the conical roofs remain in position along with the second house from the left. The three houses in the middle of the road have been replaced by the modern flats of St John's Manor. Over to the left is St John's Church.

This was built in 1857 for a congregation of the Free Church of Scotland but now serves a congregation of the Church of Scotland. The crown spire was added in 1877/78 and is a prominent landmark in Gourock. Special services were held on Sunday 16 June 1957 to celebrate the centenary of the church.

The Picture House in Kempock Place opened in 1913. Before the advent of 'talking pictures', musical accompaniment was provided by members of the Gillies family. The first 'talkie' was shown at the cinema on 14 July 1930. Hundreds of people queued to watch the film, a musical comedy called *Sunny Side Up*, starring Janet Gaynor and Charles Farrell. A report in the *Gourock Times* of 18 July 1930 stated: 'The talkies are going strong and many local people who formerly went to Greenock are now dropping in to the Kempock Place Talkie House' – presumably Greenock cinemas had still to catch up with the new technology. In 1930 admission prices to this cinema were as follows: Circle, one shilling (5p); Back Stalls, 9d (3.75p); Front Stalls, 6d (2.5p). Children

were only admitted when accompanied by parents or guardians. The Picture House closed in 1961 as a result of falling attendance figures; there was a nationwide decline in cinema attendance in the early 1960s. During the 48 years of its existence there were seven managers of The Picture House: Charles Lawson, Richard Taylor, Graham Brown, Archibald Campbell, Robert Menzies, Fred Kerr and Archie Harvey. At one time there was seating accommodation for 1,000 people but due to alterations in the 1950s the capacity was reduced to 765. The Picture House was demolished in 1981 and Gourock Library and flats now occupy the site.

On the left a small section of the Municipal Buildings in Shore Street are visible and beyond there is also a partial view of the Picture House in Kempock Place. The Municipal Buildings were officially opened on 30 January 1924. The tramlines are still in place in this view from January 1929 but by mid-July of the same year the tram service ceased to operate. The single-storey row of shops on the Pierhead are on the far right, adjacent to Kempock Street, and have since been demolished. On 7 July 1958 the Queen and the Duke of Edinburgh visited to celebrate the centenary of the Burgh of Gourock. Provost

John M. Fletcher welcomed the royal visitors outside the Municipal Buildings and then accompanied them to a platform in the gardens opposite which had been specially erected for the occasion. As part of the ceremony, Her Majesty planted a flowering cherry tree using a silver spade and then walked across the lawn to admire the floral crest which had been made with several thousand small plants. Before leaving, the Queen was presented with a bouquet of roses by Ian Fletcher, the son of Provost Fletcher, and also a copy of *The Story of Gourock 1858-1958* by Colin Milne.

This building, known as 'The Kursaal' (a German word meaning 'a hall in a spa resort'), occupied a site on the east of Station Road on which the Bay Hotel was later built. It was erected in the early years of the twentieth century as a venue for summer entertainments and roller skating. In the 1920s it was converted into a cinema known as The Pavilion. However, there were also 'go-as-you-please sessions' on a weekly basis when local people had the opportunity to demonstrate their talents at singing, dancing and comedy. One of the local performers was A. J. Gamble, who also appeared at theatres all over Scotland. The Pavilion did not show 'talkies' so it did not last long and the building once again became a roller skating rink and boxing matches, flower shows and tennis tournaments were also held there. There was even a small zoo at one time. The condition of the Kursaal deteriorated and it was demolished in the 1930s when the site was taken over by the Pierhead Development Company. The Kursaal's function as a place of entertainment was taken over by the Cragburn Pavilion from 1936. The site of the Kursaal is now open ground in front of Gourock Railway Station.

The building on the right of this view is the Bay Hotel, which stood opposite Kempock Gardens. Designed by J. W. Laird of Laird and Napier, Glasgow, the hotel was officially opened on 12 April 1938 by John Alan Burns, 4th Lord Inverclyde, who was presented with a souvenir key as a memento of the occasion. The hotel was built by the Pierhead Development Company at a cost of £20,000 and the ground floor of the building was occupied by shops and a bank. There was also a garage situated at the rear. The entrance to the hotel was at the corner of Station Road. The residents' lounge and dining rooms were on the first floor. On the second and third floors there were 34 bedrooms. There was one private suite which consisted of a bedroom, sitting room and bathroom. An interesting feature was the roof garden on the north section of the building. The hotel's cocktail bar was designed in sapele wood which resembled mahogany and a press report described it as 'modern in style and decoration with artistic tables and stools'. The building also had electric lifts. The Bay Hotel was demolished in 1999 in order that the pierhead redevelopment could take place and its site is now open space, as can be seen in the photograph on page 39.

The Bay Hotel dominates this view of Station Road from about 1940. The Picture House is visible straight ahead in Kempock Place. On the right is the domed McPherson Fountain which was then located at the junction of Kempock Street and the former Station Road. It was removed around 1940 in order that the widening of Kempock Street could take place. The fountain was gifted by Duncan McPherson (1845-1910) in the first decade of the twentieth century. In 1980 the fountain was discovered in fragments at a council rubbish tip and these pieces were 'rediscovered' in the early years of the twenty-first century when the Greenock firm of W. H. Kirkwood Ltd. won a £50,000 contract to rebuild it. After restoration the fountain was placed in Kempock

Gardens in 2005. Duncan McPherson served with the Gem Shipping Line for 40 years. He became Commodore Skipper of the Fleet and then Marine Superintendent. McPherson retired in 1904 and went to live in 'Mavis Bank' in Ashton Road. He also served as a bailie on Gourock Town Council and was a Commodore of the Royal Gourock Yacht Club. In his will Duncan McPherson left funds for a cottage hospital to be built in Gourock and the McPherson Hospital at Midton opened in 1925, providing accommodation for fourteen patients. The area seen here has been transformed into open space in front of the redeveloped Gourock Station.

SMITH'S DRAPERY STORES.

The Place to Buy Stylish and Reliable Goods.
All Your Holiday Wants Anticipated.

| HIGHEST QUALITY. | | LOWEST PRICES.. |

LADIES'

Blouses, = =
Gloves, = =
Veilings, = =
Neckwear, =
Hose, = =
Corsets, = =
Underwear.

GENT.'S

Shirts, = =
Collars, = =
Scarves, =
Hats & Caps,
Socks, = =
Braces, = =
Underwear.

| LARGEST SELECTION. | | BEST :: :: VALUE. |

PIERHEAD, :: GOUROCK.

The premises of Smith's Drapery Stores were formerly located at the pierhead which was adjacent to Kempock Street and were demolished in common with all the other properties at this location. This advertisement gives a very detailed description of the various items of clothing on sale and the business was clearly very invested in the holiday market. In the first half of the twentieth century the population of Gourock doubled and sometimes trebled during

July and August each year because of the large number of holidaymakers. Many of them were Glasgwegians, especially during the Glasgow Fair Fortnight in July. In the late 1950s there were still six hotels in Gourock. Three of them were temperance hotels (no alcohol sold), all of which were in Kempock Street. There is now a new road where the stores were located.

W. F. Wilson's business in Kempock Street was established in 1851. These premises are now occupied by Original Artists.

Some of the coloured tiles from the butcher's shop remain in position inside and the name of W. F. Wilson can still be seen on the floor at the entrance to these premises.

BATHING POOL AND WAR MEMORIAL, GOUROCK   D 27

The Bathing Pool (now known as the Gourock Outdoor Pool) was opened in the summer of 1909 in the presence of several thousand people. Renovation of the pool took place in 1935. In 1964 admission charges for the pool were one shilling for adults and sixpence for children. Season tickets cost fifteen shillings for adults and ten shillings for children. Five years later a water heating system for the pool was installed which used salt water from the River Clyde. At the end of the summer season of 2010 the pool was closed in order that a major refurbishment project could be implemented and this was completed before the end of 2011. The unveiling ceremony at the war memorial in Albert Road commenced at 1 p.m. on Sunday 11 March 1922. The Rev. G.B. Thomson officiated and Mrs Darroch, accompanied by Provost John M. Adam, performed the actual unveiling. A speech was given by Sir Hugh

Shaw-Stewart, 8th Baronet, after which many wreaths were laid on the memorial including those from ex-servicemen, the Territorials, Lieut. Col. Darroch and family, the Town Council, burgh officials and youth organisations. After the conclusion of the ceremony relatives and friends of those who lost their lives in the First World War also laid wreaths. The memorial was designed by Colin Sinclair and takes the form of an obelisk in grey granite which has a cross, laurel wreath and carved shields bearing the coat-of-arms of the Burgh of Greenock. There are 99 names of local men who died in the First World War on the memorial and 74 from the Second World War.

In 1896 plans were prepared for the construction of esplanades on the shore at both the East and West Bays. This is a view of the esplanade at West Bay which was completed in 1900. It was in 1882 when roads and streets in Gourock became the responsibility of the town council. Heavy storms had a detrimental effect as large sections of roadways were severely damaged and the construction of the esplanades prevented further deterioration. On the extreme left of this view is a cast-iron drinking fountain which no longer functions. It was erected in 1897 to celebrate the Diamond Jubilee of Queen Victoria's reign and was originally located further east on the esplanade, moving to its present location in 1938. The fountain came from Walter Macfarlane

and Company's Saracen Foundry in Glasgow. Jubilee celebrations took place in Gourock on 22 June 1897. There was a children's fete in the public park in the afternoon with a wide-ranging sports programme, and on leaving the park every boy and girl was presented with a jubilee medal. A 'high tea' was held in the Gamble Institute for 'a hundred of the aged inhabitants of Gourock', all of whom were presented with a 2lb packet of tea. The Jubilee celebrations concluded with a large bonfire being lit in the late evening on Tower Hill.

The Cragburn Pavilion was built in 1935/36 on Albert Road, on the site of the demolished Cragburn House. It was designed by J. and J. A. Carrick in brick and stucco, with art deco fluting at the front of the building, and construction cost £11,000. The formal opening by Col. A. D. McInnes Shaw took place on 16 May 1936 when Sir Harry Lauder, the famous Scots comedian and singer, became the first person to perform on its stage. There was also 'A Grand Opening Concert' two days later on 18 May. Many local bands played there, including Charlie Harkin's Kit Kat Orchestra and Harry Morrison and his Swingstars, and acts from around Britain also performed, such as Joe Loss, Oscar Robin and Lew Stone. There were also summer shows with well-known

Scottish performers, including Tommy Morgan, Alec Finlay, Larry Marshall and the One O'Clock Gang. The American comedian Jack Benny performed here in the 1950s. In the 1960s there was a decline in the big band scene but the Cragburn Pavilion continued to be used for variety shows, pantomimes and functions organised by the Town Council who owned the venue by that time. In its later years it became a cinema and a ballroom and was also used as a disco. It closed in the 1990s and the flats of Cragburn Gate have since been built on its site.

An electric tram outside the clubhouse of the Royal Gourock Yacht Club on Ashton Road. The tramline ran for 7.42 miles from Cathcart Street in Greenock to its terminus further along this road. The contract price for the Gourock section of the line was £10,000 per mile. The last three-quarters of a mile in the town were single track with three passing loops. A horse-drawn service operated from 1 July 1873 until 7 November 1901, the day electric trams were introduced. The electric trams continued in service until 15 July 1929 when they ceased operation and were replaced by buses. The Royal Gourock Yacht Club was originally known as the Gourock Sailing Club when it was founded in 1894. The club became known as the Gourock Yacht Club in 1900 and in

1908 King Edward VII was pleased to endorse it as 'Royal Gourock Yacht Club'. This clubhouse was built in 1902. James Coats of the famous thread-making family in Paisley donated funds for its construction and moored his schooner *Gleniffer* alongside the clubhouse. When King George V and Queen Mary visited Gourock in July 1920 the King presented a challenge cup to the club which was to be awarded annually, specifically 'for the smaller yachts in a class where there would be the larger number of entries and in which the industrial workers in the neighbourhood would themselves take the most interest'.

Cloch Caravan Park occupies a prominent site overlooking the Firth of Clyde, three miles south-west of Gourock. A report in the *Gourock Times* of 2 September 1960 mentioned 'the new caravan park' which at that time was operated by Trailways Ltd at the former Cloch Point Battery site. The report stated: 'During the season this has been a busy place with caravans a welcome addition to the local tourist industry'. The caravan park consists of 24 acres of mature woodland. It was used as a location in 2002 for Ken Loach's film *Sweet Sixteen* which starred Martin Compston, then a teenager. The remains of the gun battery are still visible on the shore side of Cloch Road. During the First and Second World Wars an anti-submarine boom was positioned across

the River Clyde from Cloch Point to Dunoon in order to prevent enemy submarines proceeding up river. The Cloch Point Lighthouse is situated on Cloch Road beneath the caravan park. It was designed by Thomas Smith and his son-in-law Robert Stevenson, grandfather of the author Robert Louis Stevenson. The building of the lighthouse was completed in 1797 and on 11 August of that year the first oil lantern was lit. The lighthouse was built in order to warn ships to avoid the Gantocks which is a dangerous reef of rocks directly west of Cloch Point. The name 'Cloch' is Gaelic for 'by the stone'.

Many people spent their holidays at this extensive campsite at Lunderston Bay near Gourock. Large numbers of Glasgwegians came here during the traditional Fair Holiday Fortnight in July during the decades before the Second World War. As can be seen here, the field would be packed with vast numbers of tents of all shapes and sizes. There were also several hundred wooden huts, some with floors covered by linoleum or even carpet. The camp had a grocer's, butcher's and baker's. In July 1926 a *Gourock Times* report stated the following: 'The shops do a steady trade with the campers and also with the numerous visitors which the camp attracts.'